In My O

Written by Melaina Faranda
Illustrated by Aki Fukuoka

PEARSON

Here are three issues or news stories that are about the way we live. What do *you* think? Choose one of these issues and write your opinion. Try to convince people to agree with your point of view!

Computers to replace teachers

A new report claims that computers will be used to teach school children in the future.

Professor Mary Watts says that children will still go to school and sit in a classroom. But, instead of having a teacher, they will be taught by computers. "It's very exciting," Professor Watts says. "Students will have more choices about what they want to learn. They will be able to learn at their own pace."

Bella:

In my opinion, computers should never replace teachers.

Teachers are kinder than computers. They know about our lives and care about us. When teachers are excited about a lesson, it makes learning fun. Have you ever seen an excited computer?

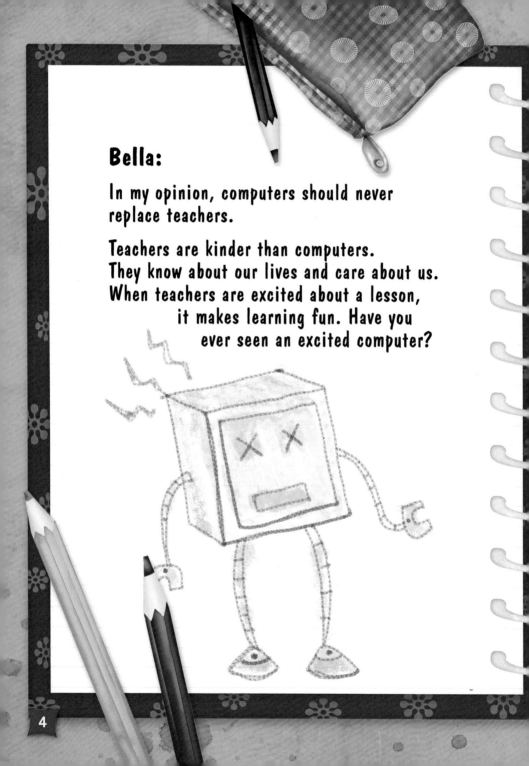

Teachers can make the
whole class work in groups
— computers can't do that.
Plus, if a kid was fooling
around, a computer wouldn't
be able to stop it! Computers
always have problems and
break down. A lot of time
is wasted waiting for
them to be fixed.

Kaleb:

I think it would be better to learn from a computer instead of a teacher.

A computer doesn't get cross or tell us to be quiet. A computer never gets tired or sick. It always remembers what page we're up to! Having the same teacher all the time can be boring. Computers have all sorts of exciting ways to teach us. They can teach us with video clips, graphics, and games.

By learning from a computer, kids would be able to work through lessons at their own pace. Smarter kids wouldn't be held back. And kids who need more time to learn would get it. Everyone would learn properly.

Keeping Pets

Animal group calls for ban on pets

An animal welfare group says that people should not keep pets. "Animals are naturally wild," says a member of the group, Cam Peterson. "It's cruel to keep pets. By making animals into our pets, we stop them from living freely. People keep pets for selfish reasons, but animals don't need us."

Therese:

In my opinion, people should not be allowed to keep pets.

Having pets is about making humans feel good instead of giving animals what they need. Animals need to be wild and free and live with their own species. How would we feel if humans were the pets? We wouldn't like being bought and sold and carted around in cages. We wouldn't like being able to eat only when someone decided to feed us.

Pets are often locked up in tiny yards, tied up, or kept in cages. People don't usually let their pets follow their instincts. They usually try to stop pets from running, digging and flying.

I think that anyone who wants to keep a pet should have to spend a day in a cage first.

Pedro:

In my view, people should be allowed to keep pets because both pets and people benefit from living together.

Keeping pets helps children learn about caring for other creatures. When I spend time with my dog, it makes me feel happy. My dog likes being with me too. He never tries to run away. I don't see why an animal would prefer to be wild. It would have to live in the cold and rain and hunt for food. It would also be in danger of being hunted by other animals. Most pets are kept warm and safe and are fed every day.

Some retirement homes keep cats because research shows that patting a pet can bring down a person's heart rate. Pets can also help lonely people live longer by being their companions.

I think that everyone should have a pet. Pets get looked after and they teach us how to care and be nicer people!

Electronic versus printed books

Electronic books to replace printed books

The head of a major publishing company says they will stop publishing printed books. Sarah Armstrong says, "It's expensive to make printed books. Readers prefer having one electronic notepad that can hold hundreds of stories. We have to accept this and change with the times."

Eva:

In my opinion, we should get rid of printed books and only have electronic ones. Having an electronic book would be like carrying a whole library in one book. People would no longer have to find room for shelves of dusty books.

Having electronic books instead of printed books means that fewer forests would be cut down to make paper. It would be an important way to help save the environment. It would also help save my shoulders. If my schoolbooks were electronic, then my bag wouldn't be so heavy!

Jed:

In my opinion, printed books are far better than electronic ones. It doesn't matter as much if a paper book gets lost or damaged because it is not as expensive as an electronic book. An electronic book can break down and its battery can lose power. But we are always able to read a printed book because it doesn't rely on technology.

Printed books feel better to hold. I like the smell of printed books. I like to touch and turn the pages. Electronic books have computer screens that can hurt my eyes if I read for too long. I enjoy having my collection of books on my shelf. If I want to find something in a printed book, I can always go straight to the page. It takes much longer to find the page I want in an electronic book.

I think that, even if there are electronic books, we should keep making printed books because they will last for longer and they are nicer to read.

15

When teachers are excited about a lesson, it makes learning fun. Have you ever seen an excited computer?

Having the same teacher all the time can be boring. Computers have all sorts of exciting ways to teach us.

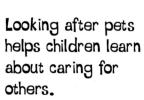

Looking after pets helps children learn about caring for others.

Persuasive Arguments

- are used to make a case for something.
- are used to change opinion.

How do you write persuasive arguments?

Step One

The writer says what the problem is:

An animal welfare group says that people should not keep pets.

Step Two

The writer gives an opinion:

In my opinion, people should not be allowed to keep pets.

Step Three

The writer explains his or her opinion:

> Having pets is about making humans feel good instead of giving animals what they need. Animals should be free to move around in their natural environment.

Step Four

The writer says what could be done:

> I think that anyone who wants to keep a pet should have to spend a day in a cage first.

Guide Notes

Title: In My Opinion...

Stage: Fluency

Text Form: Persuasive Argument

Approach: Guided Reading

Processes: Thinking Critically, Exploring Language, Processing Information

Written and Visual Focus: Speech Bubbles

THINKING CRITICALLY
(sample questions)

- What do you think this book could be about? Look at the title and discuss.
- Look at page 3. "Students will have more choice about what they want to learn when they have computers instead of teachers". Do you think this is true? Why or why not?
- Look at pages 4-5. Do you agree with the points made by Bella? Why or why not?
- Look at pages 6-7. Do you agree with the point: "Having the same teacher all the time can be boring"? Why or why not?
- Look at pages 8-9. Why do you think Therese suggests that anyone who wants to keep a pet should be locked up for a day in a cage?
- Why do you think she asks: "How would we feel if humans were the pets"?
- Look at pages 10-11. "Pets get looked after and they teach us how to care and be nicer people!" Do you think this is true? Why or why not?
- Look at pages 12-13. Do you think like Eva that we should "get rid of printed books"? Why or why not?
- What comparisons can you make about the different ways Eva and Jed think about books?

EXPLORING LANGUAGE

Terminology
Spread, author and illustrator credits, imprint information, ISBN number

Vocabulary
Clarify: issues, persuade, pace, graphics, animal welfare group, naturally wild, selfish, species, retirement homes, electronic book, technology

Adjectives: excited, smarter, tiny, nicer

Pronouns: your, they, us

Homonyms: here/hear, break/brake

Synonyms: exciting/thrilling, pace/speed

Print Conventions
Exclamation marks, question marks, apostrophes and contractions (wouldn't, doesn't)